This is normal.

Rachel Rodriguez

BookLeaf Publishing

India | USA | UK

Presentation by *BookLeaf Publishing*

Web: www.bookleafpub.com

E-mail: info@bookleafpub.com

ISBN: 9789363303119

First edition 2024

capricorn season

01.12.2021 approaching event horizon, she wrote:

This can't for on for much longer. I owe it to the both of us to just end it.

It would be another 5 months before she reached the supermassive black hole.

The red snake

When I first saw the red snake it was wrapped around the corner of my favorite couch.

This may conjure images of large luxurious lounge areas in a decadent home, with many a couch and pouf to faint upon.

You might picture me pacing the halls of each wing of my home, searching for the perfect cushion to throw my body across in a show of both exhaustion and self care.

Finally, I exclaim, "There it is! The IKEA Kivik of my dreams!" and I giddily bellyflop into the cushions.

It really did happen like that. Only it was an IKEA showroom, not a mansion that I personally own.

Anyway back to the red snake on my favorite couch.

When I first saw his tail peeking around the corner I wondered how a little snake like this could even slither its tiny body all the way into my house and up the arm of my couch.

As I rounded the corner and began to assess the situation more fully, the snake grew.

It became a large cobra and stretched the entire length of the couch. As soon as I noticed it, I called out to alert everyone of its presence.

That ole snake stood straight up when I did that! As if to let me know that it became instantly aware when I turned from curious observer to enemy. As if to let me know that knowing such a thing is even possible.

The more I worried about the snake the stronger it became, eventually morphing into a metallic red.

I knew then, that the best course of action would be to wake up from the dream I was having.

"How odd," I thought when I awoke.
"I'm not even afraid of snakes. I'm afraid of rats."

The Wizard

"and just who the hell do you think you are?"
they sneered as if it would make me shrink down
and fuck off back to Kansas

"I'm the motherfucking Wizard of Oz.
I'm the man behind the curtain,
and the bitch who pulls it back."

dream ghost of you

waking up from a dream
where some version of you
was haunting my psyche

desperately repeating
"come back to me""come back to me"
as I try to fall asleep again

knowing, as a sleepy tear
breaks over the surface
and falls to my pillow,

you won't be there.
and even when you are,
you're usually walking away.

ain't it kinda telling that
even in my dreams, you're hiding.

spotify

I don't want to see your playlists and wonder
who you think about when you carefully craft a
love score -- the soundtrack to something special
-- while I've got heartbreak's greatest hits on
repeat.

Silly sad girl, one day you'll learn, kiddo.
Well, fuck your placating tone and your use of
"kiddo".

You've proven that age doesn't mean you have a
fucking clue.

speakeasy

They'll ask me, "why'd you leave?"
and then I'll have to say
that none of those people are my friends
anbyway

and then I'll have to wait
with bated breath and pray
that the unintentional interrogation
doesn't include your name.

even him?
even him.

relief washes over because the question never
comes
but I still have to wonder about who wonders

even him? he never asked.
so the absence of your name hangs in the air, and
takes up the same amount of space as if you
were there.

speakeasy, don't leave easy.

sad girl seussical

07.02
the weight of the date
moved through me with
the force of freight

trains, how appropriate.

3 years. a slow confusing two year year taper
into silence. A year standing in the dust.

I chose it, to control the pain. As if that were
probable.
It's proving to be quite unstoppable.
these sands of time are trickling slower than I
thought possible

and guess what else?
I fucking hate sand.

sad little pen

here I am, with this
sad little pen in my hand
wondering how you'd
grade this prose

with a scowl and a pout
there is no doubt
I've cut off my face
to spite my nose

"that one little bit,
it didn't quite fit"
I'm sure you'll be the first to say.

Well I don't give a fuck
and with a little bit of luck
I'll forget your voice one day

square cows: a haiku

Wendy's hamburgers
Come from Minecraft farm raised cows
That is why they're square

dorothy: gen alpha

d: "Honestly this bitch just won't stop. It's giving
sad old spinster."
tm: "It's giving I'm gonna die alone and no one
will notice until it starts to smell."
d: "omg tinman stop, you're heartless. Toto
would definitely find her corpse before it starts
to rot. I'd bet she'd raise some hell over that."
tm: "can you raise hell from hell?"
d: "Miss Gulch could."
tm: "ummmmmmmm excuse me did you just
say her name is Gooch?"

Cat Clock

There's nothing quite like the unsettling nature of a cat clock. Functioning properly, the tail and eyes move synchronously. Inside, there is a plastic housing that connects the two. It reminds me of the inside of a toilet tank. The hypnotizing nature and constant movement of the large eyes can be too much for some folks. I suppose they don't like to wonder if their clock is perceiving them.

Before I owned a cat clock, I assumed the eyes and tail served to move the gears each time they moved together from side to side. As it turns out, however, this is achieved by two size D batteries, which seem to have a mass greater than the sum of the rest of the cat clock's parts.

Sometimes, for no reason at all, the eyes and tail will come to a stop. This is where the dreadful feelings bits about the cat clock start to creep in. You see, as unsettling as it is to wonder if your clock is perceiving you in the constant motion of its large cartoon eyeballs, it is exponentially more unsettling when they come to a stop.

The ticks continue, as if to remind us that time continues to move even when it looks like it's standing still. I find myself perplexed at how much more disturbing the cat clock is, sitting still on the wall. Initially, it was something that seemed so odd and maybe even creepy to behave in such a way, but now it is so comically wrong to be without motion that I almost cannot believe it. Looking at its rigid stillness, everything in the universe feels wrong for this cat and myself in this moment for it to be stuck still on the wall this way. It's like it's screaming, "PLEASE MOVE MY TAIL. I CANNOT EXIST IN THIS STAGNANT STATE!" Like the rotation of the earth on its axis is dependent upon every cat clock on every wall flicking its little plastic tail and staring into your soul at designated intervals.

The official brand name of a cat clock is Kit-Cat Klock. I bet the Kardashians would love that.

Alphabet Soup

everyone I know
has a favorite food
that's alphabet soup

what's your flavor?
mine's AuDHD

parenting

parenting is cool
except for all of the parts that absolutely suck
and I wasn't prepared for how much I'd be
saying,
"hey bubba, do you think you could do more
quiet pooping?"

overheard

 I was walking one morning
when I heard a man say

"When there's something to look at,
 I don't like to ogle. I like to look around"

I found it quite perplexing
because we were walking next to the ocean

Who doesn't ogle the ocean?

cloud commune

the next time
you find yourself
in the fog

consider one important thought:
you could live an entire life inside of a cloud,
and no one would know.

toy piano

the instructions to a toy piano say something to
the effect of:

"Tuning this instrument is approximate and will
likely never be exactly perfect. This adds to the
character and we hope you'll love it as much as
we do."

I plan on providing similar instructions to
anyone who interacts with me in the future.

blue eyes

how many songs
about blue eyes
never mattered before

the sight of blue
makes me feel you

curtain call

and with a long deep bow
that nobody asked for
i bid the old me adieu
along with the rest of you
who are are determined
to immortalize me as such